THE FACT OF MUSIC

THE FACT
OF MUSIC

Poems by
JONATHAN GRIFFIN

THE MENARD PRESS
1980

The publisher and the author wish to thank the editors of *Country Life, Green River Review* and *Montemora* for having welcomed some of these poems, and for permitting them to re-appear in book form.

ISBN 0 903400 49 9

The Menard Press is a member of ALP

Menard Press books are distributed in North America by SBD: Small Press Distribution, 1636 Ocean View Avenue, Kensington, California 94707.

The Menard Press
23 Fitzwarren Gardens
London N 19 3TR

Printed in England by Skelton's Press,
Wellingborough, Northamptonshire.

Like hawks we are at least not
Nowhere, and I would say
Where we are

GEORGE OPPEN

To the questions most people deeply want answered there is no undisputed answer. If there is a truth about them, the way towards it seems likeliest to be that of drama: to try if a convergence of naked reactions to the vital questions will bring us near. A play, an opera, can do this through clashes between imaginary living people: here encounters between poems may do it. Each of these poems is meant to work and please on its own; but also they interact, and the book as a whole should make sense if read straight through.

J.G.

The lay-out of the poems is not random: it contains a simple notation, useful in reading aloud. A line with 5 stresses starts fairly near the left-hand edge of the page, one with 4 stresses further to the right, one with 3 the same distance further, and so on: a reader who is unsure how many stresses to make in a line has only to observe where it begins.

This system of indentation is strictly maintained, with (in this book) one exception — the poem on page 68, which is a quotation from an earlier work.

Some other (and normal) expression-marks, such as breaks in a line or enlarged spaces between lines or between words, are also used, but freely, as the form requires.

J.G.

CONTENTS

I

I had a vision, once.
                    Of what?

        In a wood, a young birch —
    leaves just out, against light blue —
I stopped on the path, looking.
                    Then a change
(in me, I suppose). It was a vision: I saw

                    the tree
Not as a symbol or image or embodiment
of a being or thing read or heard of Not (say)
a nymph (though I may have felt it as feminine)
I saw the tree iself   As itself
in its own shape
                Yet I was seeing godhead
                    (did feel that then)
My eyes seeing the godhead of a tree

                I had to go,
                not be late home.

                The place again,
                several times —
                the tree was there,
                I did not see.
                    There was
                nothing to say
            (I learned this when I tried).

        The modest holy tree
may have come in here made me wait and want
                to be a poet
                    when
                    true

An unknown language
        is best to listen to —
danger of understanding
        probably lessened

        and if you did
        listen too hard
        you will pretend
not   to understand

        persuade even
        yourself you never
                heard
the irreversible word

                A poet
                heard it

                dared
                show it

MUTE FAULT
for Raymond Tyner

Louise Homer   heard
            the San Andreas Fault
        'suddenly split apart
(. . .) tearing the earth and buildings and emitting
a shrill (. . .) wail, like a thousand off-tune violins,
(. . .) crescendo of shrieking cymbals and whining cellos,
                        a weird
            orchestral din
                    that flooded
        the region (. . .), then ceased abruptly, leaving (. . .)
                    a smoldering (. . .)
                silence'

And James Hopper, a reporter from *The Call,*
                    saw
'many men and women with grey faces.
All of them had a singular hurt expression
— not (. . .) of physical pain, but rather (. . .) injured
                sensibilities,
as if some trusted friend had suddenly wronged them
        or (. . .) someone had been rude (. . .)'

Divested of divinity Earth dying
                under the final fall-out
Each leaf is its own cross nailed to the sky . . .

Stillness — one should be hearing the fault cry

                the fault on high

All my trees
            war cemeteries
                        quaked wry

Note   The quotations are from 'Louise Homer and the Golden
Age of Opera', by Anne Homer.

17

Come out at night
tunnelling soul
to drink the hill
dew —
            mole
daring the frontier of the owl

            not
            far
        and listen for
    the wings of the patrol

            Bare
        hill-top and
    the dew
            and dewsweet air

        The impended open

LULLABY

Everychild!
        You
        must be
our enemy:

a tokyoid world
        we
        leave you
t'be born into.

APPEAL

Neuter Moon
Earth's one
perfect desert —
death quintessenced

warn Her of Man

The E-string of a violin can make
                         my throat   ache
Do trumpets rouse us through our sinus nerves —
                         bright in us, knives?

The child Mozart staggered as the edge hacked him.

All
runs

away
until

time — asymptotic to eternity —
shall
have made the perfect landing / have run still

Time will
end
as
(is)
entropy
endless
level
omnidimensional
runway

Music is made

of the enemy

— time itself:

music makes

from entropy

volumes, love.

Sleep is a hearing and not listening

>   Our lidless ears
>   until
>   death-
>   earlids
>   seal us deaf

Listening? To wake and wake: ears watching, life

To meet and not evade a work of art
is
   in a grown man
           the next adolescence —

           To grow, men shelve
           their early selves —
then fruit-fresh honesty-at-last art confesses
    those as they were. Adult it faces
          the youth's questions, which are.

The provocation of great music is;
　　　　　some sweet music rebukes.
　　　Because it is,　　says *Why not?*

　　　　　　　You heard it says
　　　　　　　Keep faith　　*Cease*
　　　　　　　to acquiesce

　　　Faith　　*with*　　*Earth!*
　　　　　　　　cries
　　　music the reminder of
　　　　　　　love
　　　　　　　Praise!
　　　　　　　Praise
Earth the sense and voice of the Universe —
　　　　　　　　rare
　　　　　　　tuned held truth
　　　　　　　water and breath!
　　　　　　　Praise
　　　　　　　and spare!

The fact of music — once known, how deny it?

　　　　　and in the silences
　　　　　still　　*You heard* it says

II

ASKED WITH AWE

                    Trendy
                    Humanity,
        is
          air obsolete?
        Earth   out of date —

          windjammer planet?

THE SUN'S LOVE WON
for Linda Gutièrrez

The Sun in person sits and sings
on the trees' shoulders in green wings . . .

Spread, they stay —
called to life
and held as leaves
by Orpheus light

till (daysong shortening) leaves die
and then
fly

Where they hang   the pluck of day
closes yellow and red

In the brown dead
the Sun in person
stoops
and grieves . . .

An autumn-end — the robin-coloured trees
and soon simply the long boughs of winter
— storms gutting — calms that merely freeze . . .
Vulnerable weather, wild resurrection wonder!

sensitive tissue of fugitive balances
roofless always and now withered from under
      by roofed warmed man greed without cease
        infiltrating the winds.

Man thought he'd conquer Nature and he has
      changed Nature into Man — who is
          more treacherous than weather
than God — Man is the worldwide manmade weather
to end weather —
        end life with it —
                scorch Earth:
the treachery of all gods put together.

As being in love
brings the whole world alive
Earth
fills
the diffusing Universe
with sense

as long as She is there
freighted with water
with green and air

Future?

The All
neuter

too many Man
fallen
out of love

WITH AWE, BLUNTLY

Earth, Who alone could give
green tongues to the Sun,
Who (more-than-mirror) return
to the Sun answers which live,

Goddess!
    will Man
        find grace
    soon
to exterminate his own
    race
not drag the green givers of breath
    with him to death?

Grass is holy
        cattle holy
             The sea's
grass — the first pasture, also largest source
       of sweet air which the rootless need —
sea's light-eating fields are the Holy of Holies

          Many lives   are
          sacred Not most the human

               What does Man feed?
does Man shine any light? do we excrete
                pure air?

             Man
             is greed
             freed

The open Holy of Holies the sea's fields —
              fishes drowned,
        auk gannet sea-mew oiled
        on the spoiled spawning-ground,
           the plankton killed:
Manspillage spreading deserts — Man, the wild
well —
        cap it, pinch it shut! tamp it with mud
                to save
                the sea
           for life's sake

'All lives are sacred'? No, for life is sacred

THE INNOCENTS
for Eliot Weinberger

The grazers of the green plains of the seas
— the innocent holy copepods — have weight
yet so   little — upheld by friction, easy
they nose   just under   hang from water

by plumes,   featheriest lazily raised
antennules (gold / or bronze / or iridescent) . . .
all of which, when they quake and jerk to flee,
trail   in friction trap them: prey-in-waiting.

Their lives are sacred, deaths gracious — their delvings
do no   harm, do clear good, pass the food-chain
on,   pure, to the fishes — who sustain

                    dolphins.   Earth! save clean
the almost weightless sustainers of the meaning —
Quick! before hominids poison the dolphins!

THE HOPES OF VIRUSES

                Amoeba collides-includes.
                    Sperm hopes
                    smells that have shapes?
How does a virus find its way to foods?
by scent? or from betrayer tremors as
cattle know in their hooves the coming quake?

            To sniff cooking   is osmosis
                    Pure air breathed deep transforms us
                    A smelled rose is
                            a light
that brings the absent girl into deep sight

The hopes of viruses — some: self-dooming greeds
        like us   Self-cramming to breed
                    self-famining hordes
                        we
                are members of a pest

            Infested Goddess home!
                    host!
        have pesticidal mercy — shake
                        free
                from this beast

The windy planet with the pink sky —
　　　　　global dustbowl . . .

　　　　　Be its double?
blue and white Earth by Man nibbled dry?

Man was not expelled
from Eden, is degrading it to hell

Take,   heart,
         a hard
look at God

and turn away
         to pray
Earth get rid

SALVATION

Winter dusk, ineffable lavender . . .
For a timely extinction Earth sighs grace —
the folk, the green givers, will take the place —
whole horizon bowls of Avatar . . .

The turn of Man the Black Death to move under
came just in time
                            to save the airgiver grass
and callous healing oceans for at last

ablution and the rose-of-the-winds scavenger.

An epidemic when it falters is Nature
cutting the next burst population down
(one more wave of ecstatic lemmings drown):

a plague is two Black Deaths — it, and its own.
The death of a disease is a disaster,
this self-sown horde reaping what it has sown.

Transgalactic compassion?
flickers across parsecs,
the waved handkerchief stars —

The dead Moon strikes stone luminous, dims (to Earth)
the stars

Eyes that must see mercy in a Black Death!
— that thought
is a serrated dark, a statue's
shadow crinkled across a flight of steps

III

Evil and Good plain

Greed Man in power over Earth the Good
— if I believed in God I should curse God!

Must find if I can
why not to curse Man

In   the scattering Universe
of the stars' hurtling furnaces

among the planet pinnaces
       will
         — of the very likely
other worlds laden with life
       (our company
               each instant
               more distant) —
       One

          evolve
          delphinic
     lords   too wise to
     lay Her   waste?

TEST

> What is it a man believes in?
> Find to what he gives
>
> Free   a man will give
> the years which make a self
> that a son of his may live
> to become one more slave

NINE PLUS

> One rëal thing is   the faith-need:
> killed by Church after Church   God
>   has more lives than a cat

ARE THEY COMING?

> It's been a long
>   drought
>
>   Along
> the decorated street
> souls   dogs' tongues   hanging out

REVEREND

Enough lies!
God is abjection
old age adopted under fear of death —
one could

despise
God
respect
every man and woman aware of death.

EPITAPH FOR A SCIENCE

The child would explore
the spider's trap-door

THE PRIMITIVES

Men who set science free
showed faith in God —
they trusted God to see
that truth be good.

FACT

It's a good joke
it isn't funny

Give a belly
laugh   feel sick

A LAUGH OF GHOSTS

Ghosts rise after exorcism alive
instead of vanishing — with newborn candour
use their long held breath
                              to confirm the smile of
the tiger on the face of the Gioconda

OVER POLAND, 28TH AUGUST 1939
for Anthony Rudolf

Across those wheatfields
                              which the early sun
is moulding exquisitely
                              dimples run:

(seen from the air) shell-holes of World War One

47

Forest   felled   soil   gone
rock without shapes   grey   brown
        Earth
    in evermourning
       for the
victories of men

    progress of disease —
      with a half life
      to outlast life
    the enveloping effluent
        men
fouling their antipodes

now is worse than any then —
mountain snow
      glacier water
    begin to be tainted
Icebergs are being born
      dirty

AGAIN AFTER?

The clear Thief   steals up   and the flames
fade into the Lord on a face of water —

birch torches on a many-falled stream   men
              few again
                        spearing salmon

GET THE SCENE —

                              the scene is
                    after the goats
                    Man
                              nibbling
                    Earth soon
              sahara & dead sea

Believe?   No. Half hope

For — ?

That those who love
                    meet again whole

Doesn't one fear?
Hell the remorse looking from beyond death
at what we did to Earth

— poem by Bronk, and in it
he says 'of what we discern perhaps there could be
to tell that we know too little except it is there

and not in us, not by us: good
or evil, it does not matter what we do.'

It does
We
matter because we are dangerous
to
what matters and is
not us

It matters to not reduce
Earth to another Moon
It matters at least that Man
should become extinct before   he
extinguishes life
That the life of
the sea should survive Man, the leaf
kill itself for the tree

EELS ARE WORTH A CHEER

Eelsilver! strike out, down
— still — to the deep sea's open dark
until
the Effluents
take
and contraceive your spawning-grounds.

UFO MESSAGE?

A lense in air,
a phoenix eye —
galaxy
shape, only near:

*Man has no
right to be here*

52

Jesus died
unshriven
wanted not absolution but belief —
the hope to wake in Paradise with the thief
and not have lied

There must be
the St. Barbara mercy —
the inclusive sacrament she
has rushed to Noman'sland and
given
with her still chainmail-gloved hands to the thirsty

YOU WHO AVOID THE ISSUE,

I know I ought not to avoid the issue
               And why be mealy-mouthed
          and not use the great words
                       when they
            are what I have to say?

Why call a spade a spade and not God God?
        Why talk freely of what a body
               does to a body
         and shrink to speak of souls?

of saving God-surviving holiness?

            or doom
                   since the issue is
                life and death?

        Why not mention the Universe
             which is where we are living?
Why not call by name and look in the face
                Earth
           Whom we are killing?

SMILING JANUS

Humour — the harmless form of shame — keeping
shame from getting morbid
                        or the creeping
           excuse for not acting on shame —
                        two-faced Humour —

                        which, this time
                        (joke the same)?

THE LOCK OF THE OPEN

                Doubt
                        key to the truth
                truth
                        my doubt's key —
                                truth is
                what fits a man's doubt
                unlocking?
                        locking?
                                Each?

The sea's self is Earth's longest broadest caverns:
zenith Sun crushed in weight of water height,
          the vaulting is Earth's curve.
Under blue,   everdark: the deep.

        Minds waked free
                inhabit
        a heavy open
     like the dark of the sea

    There is   only living light.

Why should I crush this cockroach when I've
not killed one of
the directors of the Genocide Corporations?

Marxism has become
the people's opium

addict people   freed
from hunger into greed

to take home more and more
bread but   not air or
                    light

workers as strikers Ye shall know them by
        their denied fruits
                        their strike's bite

                    sport of labour
                    bite my neighbour

    devaluation of each life

                    Did soul survive on free
                    infant mortality?

Whoever has
power for long
shows what he is
and does not see it

sees it wrong
and bends to be it

Exception bring
Man's rarest flower
hidden king
the pure in power

Posterity of poor!
if   compassion were power
and I could drive this cry   through

and past the crumbling babels comfort you

and you in new proud rage
spit on this page

Dark wake —
              helix-true
          furrow
                   raw trough
driven twisted open left

Sharp love —
              rusted share
wiped bright by laying bare

Soul! You! like most,
asleep at your post!
quick — for there is
some mercy — arise,
on pain of age!

The mercy is this start
awake of the heart

the duty of lonely seeing

the pride of being
still *adsum* and young rage

Minced fine, a sponge will breed,

Stem hides in a seed.

Can intricate men and women
fast out manmade world famine?

THROUGH THE SOUP
for Anita Barrows

In the making, sometimes, a poem is
        caterpillar in chrysalis —
                tissues break down, flow
                    — a soup: no
                parts.
                            Slow
        eddies solidify
        to (new, more intricate, the invis-
ibly inherent structure) butterfly —

A STUMBLE IN A WOOD
for Helene Koon

The bared part of this tree's root is
a quite long rod — straight until it
claws into the earth.

A root, a shape of grasping — a root is an
open,nailed down as form — a leaf is
the form of a groping for light — today
I see
all organic forms
whether
wild life or achieved in art
or yes a work of political compassion
pushed through —
each a resolved groping: either
a root or a leaf

or between these   the stem the bough
made by leaves and saved by leafdeath —
stems and branches are the drawn sculpture
the Sun's wire.

Forms
of tensions
between a seed and the light.

Without freedom
          no virtue
If no   evil
          no freedom

Does then freedom
justify evil?

Only freedom

or ends itself —
          leaves
evil free?
          Is free to

DOUBLE STANDARD

Act the duplicity which Christ taught — render
to Caesar those things that are Caesar's *and*
to God the things that *are* God's
                              so
                                   Endure
war and not hate the enemy (hate is surrender)
Fight against evil and
                    love the evildoer

And put one's good out to the Christblest usury
the living talent it is death to bury

LOCOMOTIVE-DRIVER

Here comes the mob train on the trembling track

                    And he in night
                    alone with weight —
four hundred lives inert against his back

                    Virility
                    motherly

METTLE
for Louis and Annette Kaufman

Mesh of stresses where jarred crystals have stored
          strains — a metal is
              reproach recorded,
              biding:
                    tired,
              takes the retarded
      vengeance — creeps   cracks
                snaps

In a live mind mettlesome memory uses
              strength from bruises

FREEDOM

Man's freedom is to hang like a bell, free
To shudder, not to flee:
Tethered to testimony, the free man
Cannot escape: answer is all he can,
Answer each blow, out of the well of tone
That is his own.

(from *The Hidden King*, '53)

68

TO HOLD PEACE
for Lawrence Pitkethly

No-one's free all the time, yet people have
freedom: because we need both company
and solitude (more or less half and half),
a free man's one who is fairly often free.

Open to interdependence, at times he
can *hold his peace* — gaze at one sight, receive
music, choose from the world his company
by reading — and so hold the more to give.

Obscenity is intrusion — no great evil
perhaps a nuisance. But much intrusion is an
inquisitorial evil (and obscene),

for your/my privacy matters more than even
sharing free speech. To be free to say nothing
is the life of the freedom to say anything.

OWN QUESTION
for Judith Thurman

Horn-hearted as a journalist reporting
                    his own question the words
which ripped the dressings off a victim's wounds
the obvious question stridently repeating
                    a secret to the winds —

oceankilling oil   forestuprooting
lust   fouled air soil lost
                              ask
                              Waters! woods!
the Grace of Earth and every love   parting?

A man who questions all things is by all
put to the question Mocking racking call
one's own question echoing From what wall?

One is that wall
                    And all around is
                              I'll
look hard hold my eyes open   to be able
to see with eyes shut what a thing might feel

IV

FULL FRESH
for Mark Linenthal

                    In this part
                    of the breathing world
this year the Spring came as I've never seen —
the longer light nourished it, days of rain
many on end and more days of mere grey
             retarded it, in one   day in
                        mid   May
                        it burst

        Full spread of leaves and still the first
                        green —

                    the Sun shone
                    broad
                        on
whole woods with new all sail unfurled —
        the clean start of the world

OPENCAST
for Brenda Rudolf

Clouds   moving off   bright —

now at the shine after the rain
the grass goes deeper into green
and furrowed fields show veins of height

JULY, A STRIDE OF BREEZE

Here come windsteps   blurring
the tops of the trees, curving
the tips of the straight grasses

— there — there the crops moving
aside   bowing murmuring
as a windfootfall passes

74

OUTLET

             Here the demure pool
    edge   frays
                     into dropped stitches
                 of water bolting

GUEST IN APULIA

And strolling through that garden I caught sight
             of   the persimmon tree

                    approached
                    did not touch
                    (was a guest)

stood   eyes memorising the delight

              went   blessed

DAPPLE ELEMENT
for John and Wendy Trewin

Trailed in the daystream
shadows are eddies

when a wave breaks
it turns a vertical
eddy — trundled on edge

Each
shadow
each caught gleam
is Time made cyclical
— momently complete

Things are coagulated eddies

And lit
stones   grassblades   trees   beasts   hills
clouds
cast
shadow eddies   and
wave-rings of light

Despair has prevented praise, but praise shall rise again
        beyond despair I will praise here and now

the ordered tones and intervals of the raindrops — how
                            each drop belongs
            to one of the numbered magnitudes (double the last
                and half the next, with none between)

            and praise the reason: droplets descending spin
                some clockwise others widdershins
which opposite revolving   draws together pairs
of drops — but only the equal, which sink at the same pace.
So the liquid lapse is a fabric — the bricks of the rain build
            the First Temple the portal rainbows, one
                    for each lifted-up gaze.

                            And let no despair
                                stop
                    praise for the human ear
                    staker of music — picking
out of the welter of waves   octaves and simple scales
        and from them forming a pride of rainbows glancing.
                    Man — ear — word
                    that builds with the bricks of the rain!
            Angels tread that ladder, dancing

                        *

            Rough hexagons are a common
                    result of stresses meeting —
                    each of the workers swells
                    his clamped cell
                                until
    — geometry of jostling — the wax froth sets.

Pappas of Alexandria, though, believed that the bees   chose
                the hexagonal cell   knowing
    this would enclose most honey in least wax,
          and desert Basil (forgetting the stings)
    imagined that the bees were monks and wise.
    Man put beauty into honeycombs,
    religious love gave to the bees its wisdom.

    In a froth / in a honeycomb/ in a mind
          the outer cells' outward surfaces
          curve   smoothly — the inter-faces
               pack, polyhedral, pointed.
          O seeking senses, locking logic,
          pressing cells pressed to prisms
              to make a mind! what light
          shall pierce your dark, suffuse your night?
          what light is bright for you to break
    to splinter into splendour as you eat
    to drink its singleness only to pour
          (shattered yet whole and though caught pure)
          out through crystal simplicity
          spectra true to complexities?

                  *

          Angels prefer, for all their wings,
          the ladder — the bright bridge that springs
               more soaring from
               a human dream.
    Feet   than fanning feathers far more light
               descending! fleet
          flames of pentecostal feet
          upon the risen silver rungs
    between a hushed soul and the singing height!

*

Chaldean seekers constellated the stars —
which our undoing doubt
                    shows as one cosmic rout . . .
                    Age of reverence without
                    faith — not praying, to praise.

Dextrorse and sinistrorse torsion — weaned and grave
the proportioned drops calling their equals as they fall —
                    affinities of turning love —
the seven terraces, the spectrum, hang in every speck
                    gardens beckoning . . .
                                        O take —
                    quick! — your babylon turn,
glad — though the fall be faster the splash at the end little higher —
to have reflected more of the primal light returning:
                    refracted it to kind fire.
        Bricks like eyes   that eyes on Earth may make
                            suddenly burn —
courses of colour on high — the thin arch crossing the sky

                    Make the final silence
                    a silence after music

                                            ('56/'77)

'If the Sun and Moon should doubt
they'd immediately go out' —
                    outgrown:

                    Man
        grown up
                    required to doubt
            and not go out

Live
in person — lips
and tongue touching a fipple —
fingertips unstopping, stopping —
plucking
bowing
striking
holding

Celestrial thing, an organ should still puff
— tracker action can be enough,
its clatter
does not (within reason) matter

Live
in person or at one remove

OF THE NATURE OF THINGS
for Casper Wrede

> Matter — holes, nearly all of it:
> 　　　　　　　at least there, room

> Wanted: in between men, some of
> 　　　　　　　the void in the hard

> The next men will have to create
> spiritual space inside world crowd

> each an unintimidated
> mind　　　which　　　surrounded unbinds
> — is
> 　　　　a holding apart field

> though so　　　small that　　　being warmed or cooled
> is to be in a mob — whirled held —
> and shone upon is shouted at
> in a great cave of scything rainbows

INNER NYMPHS

As woodlands are haunted our bodies hide
                    the Blood Stream
                    nymphs
                            the Haemads

vigilant the white and the red nymphs of
                    rivers of life

IT DID

                    The bursting sap   thins —
                            effort
                            after
                        integrity
                            has found
                            its end —
            the recantation honesty

                    On   the bush of thorns
                sovereign the rose burned.

GOLD RUSH

In lust with   a fortune
orbs of unrest our eyes
quarry the ore of skies

      wash the mountain
      sift   night's
      dust of lights

A THING THEY DID
for Claudine Gnoli

Climb a high place, lie down, hope for a dream.
      Some hill formerly holy
      where rites performed duly
formed the deep heavens to an echoing dome . . .

Let sleep come — you may hearken a dream home.

Man 'cannot live by bread alone' — that's right:
has to have breath as well, and inward light.
Élite is necessary
                    to create
and keep up
                    free souls' air and light, above
the greed and flattening dictatorship of —
a profiteering proletariat?

          Better a multiple standard than
          — middling and mean — one that is none.

               Both to earn daily bread
               and to make room for breath —
               and (with luck) win a right
                         to give some light.

               Now   before too late
let us found the next generous élite —

          Earth's rescuers   the pure élite
                                   the one
élite any may join
                    — of us all, no-one
can be pushed out except by own unworth

Open élite the saviours of Earth

CAEN, 1945
for Frances Jaffer

Palms will ride a storm best of all trees —
the slim fronds admit and *reconduisent*
blast as well as breeze

Standing in a
city laid
flat

Gothic ruins

Each Gothic ruin wide enough has a wooden
hat The other roofs are of
shanties in rows between house-stumps — shelter
not for people (they live in cellars):

for cafés, laundries, hairdressers' In a flat city
a woman's soul is a simple feeder — finds
its   food
in the body's food and
nice hair and the clean white shirt of pride

CHARTRES

When to
know
opens
wonder

Feeling at one
go

the golden
ratio   from end to end
of the cathedral's glow-robed skeleton

I believe — not in God, I do believe in
the glory of God, which men pay out and spin
       — the spirit's spider-silk —
       and stretch and discipline
to a law web   greater than them   bright-
doubting them with its thrown spans and caught light.
The glory of God is rëal, is what we
make from the need of it, to do and be
       our best for. As if He
       existed to receive it.

Not that caught light's what sends the taut net harping
rainbows of splinters so: a living thing
       struggles — one wing still
       clear but the other wing
stuck — until stung numb, then devoured. A flight
stumbled. Jerks of agony break some light
to a fluttering Iris swansong — it is prey
keeping the clinging filaments asway . . .
       Twitched silk glancing gay,
       the subfusc weaver hoping.

EVENRISE
for David Pinner

The land
stunned by noon

Through boiling air's vibration
at last a sign
quivers?
Again none

One
lackshade
stupor

As though sudden
standing
vesper-sharpened
the risen shadows

THE COMMON RESSURECTION

To face the fall of all gives no protection
                        from resurrection —
life is to rise again until we die

                        not know   try
protected for exposure
                        in despairing
                        sow   new daring

CÔTE D'OR

                        For the exposed toil
            choose a stony soil

                The austere vine
    yields the velveted wine

TRUE GUISE
for William Alfred

'And the catharsis fades in the warm water of a yawn' —

         'dammit, I know
              But this is
after that
        and out of doors:
             a beyond-
      tragedy, lived catharsis.

REVOLT AND DREAD

      The too keen vision cataracted blind?
               the mind
        drained?
           Not yet And I
      not to be resigned!

— unless my body strikes me as good as dead
and leaves me half-alive. That I do dread.

Lord Chandos learned at the front that 'in war all
front-line officers are of the same age,
whether they are forty or twenty, because
they are all the same distance away from death.'

       War or peace, in old age
— with luck, no stroke — one is   learning to die
young
     never let one's death get overdue

       In a day by day new
       working life   make sure
       my death be premature

A HUSH

Two living heads bending over a death
                have heard in their held breath
                                speak
a hair's parenthesis on a dead cheek

Why do I want
to go on living
and   want
to die with dignity?

Do
want the two —
working for
them   seems to make sense
even though   and more because
I can't
know that there is
a sense

Must
accept death, never agree to age —
to die with dignity one must
die young

I want to die young
having lived long —
the older the better if only
still young

the full

Stealthy drinker of sea
Sun in the cold sky

Warmth from the clear   my
doubt   higher than me

ARTHUR SCHNABEL

Alone with him on a train journey I asked
                    What is music? He answered

                The conflict of form and freedom

        and   that when he sat down to play
                    a great Schubert sonata
        he had not settled which of thirty
                    distinct interpretations
        (each of course realising all
                    Schubert's indications)
                        to try, that day

Boldest teacher and player he was afraid
                    to practise much — feared
        virtuosity insidiously
        smoothing spontaneity,
narcissism edging in front of music

Imagine a new freedom and imagine
its own form to convey it and immediate
                    a fresh freedom to burst
                        this
                            never let
                freedom   get dispersed
                    a form   set

                            *

                Often he would say
                *I want to play   only
        music which   is better than me*

                        The music he wrote
                            was way out

*

Years later I heard Lotte Lenya tell
     how   one evening at Kurt Weill's
     they had been strenuously discussing
          a revered pianist's recital
and Schnabel (eagerest talker) had said nothing . . .
               — chaffed
          said at last
      I didn't like it . . . He has such a
        noisy spiritual life

        Schnabel played as if
hearing — then — the composer show the way

Split root-holds for the life rage,
    smile-forcer erosion!
let carving water   having frozen
    thaw
        ways
            open
for claws of saxifrage

crack, rockface! admit hope's
obstinacy of self-sown herbs

That is the bell   tolling
What now shall tolling tell?

The passing bell tells of one not yet dead
who has begun dying — 'the passing bell
                     otherwise the soul-peal
. . . rung while the sick lay in extremity
                     to admonish those who heard it
                     to pray for the soul   while
                             it was passing'

After Auschwitz, poetry? Yes, the strife
to celebrate Earth while She still has life

not one   bell   tolling
                             but peals of bells
the soul-peal for
                     Earth —
                             many full peals
inter-relaying / so a perpetual
soul-peal torrent —
                     the pouring bells!
                                     pulse
                     in every head
          Pause   Pause   Pause
passer-by! and decide 'She shall not pass'

'The universe is large: to be eccentric
is to be nothing. It is not   worth
      speaking of', — Bronk.
               Something is worth
the speech of us eccentrics, namely: Earth.

To be Earth patriots
          is to become not nothing,
Earth being of the Universe not the centre
        but
           the sense

SOMEONE'S STUDY
for P. K. Page

This wintersilvering untidiness
old-man's-beard of books all over the place

fruits that have plumes
                for   a wind to disperse

            Sown by the air
            flower afar
flying silver serpent

In London again, in the Thames   fish   breathing

Rhetoric is in itself not insincere —
can mean to speak up. I
                   shall:
                            Want a cause
that unmakes the corruption of the best
and gives our lives a meaning? I have it, here:

the cause of the from now on most oppressed
                   class   your/my successors.

Workers and capitalists of the world! unite!
           not — as now — to be their oppressors.
                Unite to lift at least
                        part of their plight —
       part-disinherit them of blight.

                         Cease
treating children as enemies — no! worse!
dropping your children as industrial waste.
End that — the rëal — classwar by the first
                  classless society,
                  generations embracing:
not desert continents in one dead sea . . .

               Make, with your children, peace!

To partly free
          Earth's self-healing
                  Earth bless us!

A NEED

Cows (if they can) turn from a new-sown pasture
to old fields and wild hedges — which look poorer —,

                    or (fenced from these)
nibble the barks of trees — will kill the trees:

men to old towns, rough country. Some true need
seeks out a tangle of deep-rooted weeds

                    and (baulked) destroys.

EXERCISE

Now and then one must
rest
from shame Let us
rest
in the past (seeing we are at least
guiltless of nearly all the past)
and so rebuild the strength to face the present
in which we are
greatly guilty of the future

Rest in the beauty of
the past — preserve it
Search the present for its
beauty — deserve it
Build strength to own here now shame for the future

we   guilty in advance   traitors
to the next men — their worst predators

Learn from the evils of the past
present evils reduced
Learn from the plunder-&-poison present
the children's hell to be lessened

Live to cure of us

THE CURVES OF LIVING
for Kathleen

Cloudy sunny in deep Suffolk
a day of rest
rest from streets   from quadrilaterals
rest   hours   grazing
down lanes between
wildflowerthickets

bulbous hedgerows

trees — spheres   lifted

rest for eyes   exercising
loving near and wide
living things   curving

From lattice matter, curves of living!
the poles of the grasses halfway pliant

leaves — lifted eddies

the boles of the trees   led to labyrinth
by histories of the pulls of winds
and pulls of — generations — the sunlust
green the upward hungers

Above
this
dog-rose hedgerow
an oak round-shouldered like a lutanist

Strip
a cow —
that is, milk her
clean   leave   no
afterings in the dug to hatch disease —
curling hand charm out
the creamy strockings.

Poet!
strip

I feel I am
one of the next

and must   from
in me
                ex-
tend a light of room

There used to be a time between
            reaping and threshing, when
the host of the corn was fields of gold
            tents, many tipped with black —

from (it seemed) every other stook
            a crow craned keen
before the mechanised attack
            and judgement — barn — stack.

No stooked interim now, but in some
            — still — of the fields the bravest
solemn aftermath: straw, rolled,
            waiting — big gold drums —

                  across a hedge
                  you see
                              a henge
            of the gold drums of harvest.

V

SUSPENSION
for George and Mary Oppen

An evensigh of leaves

And now across the track there moves
a light baritone din   of sheep's hooves

This evening as though it sealed   world peace —
            evil beautiful / virtue generous:
virile — opposed still —   mazed by a truce

This air smells as though of the rose
whose petals the Sun dropped

                            Shadows raise

            blue wings

                        as though to fold
            Earth   in Her release

Night   black Book of Hours
scattered with small gold flowers

rout of enormous fires
widening nothingness

Syrinx soul   stilled   wings folded
                                    shield

    in her body's brown bower lies
    the clutch of love
             small oval skies

WHAT DOES ONE KNOW?
for Mark Kirschen

. . . much that is not measurable, as well,
                                        is

Feelings are rëal
                And some feelings tell
                        presences —

        rocks   leaves   clouds   rëal

                — may   from them   tell
                        hierarchies

A living creature out among things has
a needle on a dial in a soul

An animal's corpse smells evil —
animals die against their will.
Leaves dying and dead leaves have a good smell

       it says that all is well
because the death is their choice — sacrifice
                  to the tree —
      life's price
   paid
       willingly

           *

      'It is well that they should die,
      lest they begin to undo
      what they have   so well done.

         But before they die
   they surrender (. . .) all the residue
        of their industry
          that is worth having (. . .)
A gentle current of sugar and more complex things
(. . .) ebbs from the dying leaf into the stem (. . .)

The leaf, useful in dying as well as in living,
         becomes more and more empty
          of all but waste (. . .)
         Across the base
of the leaf-stalk, in a region which is
normally firm and tough, there grows inward

a partition of soft juicy cells, (. . .) a springy
cushion, which either foists the leaf off
or makes the attachment so delicate that
a gust of wind will soon   snap the bridge
    binding the living and the dead.'

J. Arthur Thompson, *The Biology
of the Seasons*. (And he added: 'This is fine
surgery, that the scar should be ready
                              before
                the operation is performed.')

Sainthood (some report) smells of violets.

                              *

                          What leaves
                          leave is
                    a tree alive

                    wood which leaves made
                    and leafdeaths saved —

            ancestral leaves not dead
            in wood their dying saved
                          — they died and have
                          life in
                    their deaths preserved
                          as
tall coaxial channels of saved life

                          And the leafmold
                                floods
                                shield
                    bulb and seed

                              *

Deciding the deciduous, wind of ice —
the air visible, tawny! air is leaves!
convulsive — torn off — on the run — which stumble
to plummet yet start up as if the ground

smoked
      and seem hung again bough-high
                                        jigged round
sucked millrace-straight
               dropped again
                          harrowed
                                humbled

                      *

The sibilance of the mute mouths of the leaves
shaming us   the preaching of the leaves

those undebasers building wood and breath —
fierce mother leaves — natural suicide —
nearly each leaf a saint and suicide

How holy are the sources of the breath

               Greater love
         hath no man than a leaf
              which   to save
       the tree   kills itself

       mothers to their mother

               *

       Have I no tree?
       What tree but Earth?
       Avert Her death!

What can avert it? Only She?

Sometimes I am the tree I see —
I am watching through my leaves
Earth being killed
                    am love which grieves

Mother   shed Your human leaves

                    *

A wind of the high hills ends
in nets of valley oakwoods, and
stirs
        softly
                the Fall air full of
the good smell of the suicide of leaves

The scale of the Universe makes sense by proving
            that size — alone — is nonsense

You
& I
have
for finding holding giving

the scale of values way of life prescribed by
Earth's rarity and the fact of music

JONATHAN GRIFFIN

JONATHAN GRIFFIN was born in Sussex in 1906. He was a journalist and writer on military matters before the Second World War. During the War he was Director of BBC European Intelligence and after the War a diplomat in the Paris embassy. Since 1951 he has devoted himself to writing and translating. He lives in London.

POETRY
The Hidden King (a verse trilogy) Secker & Warburg, 1955
The Rebirth of Pride Secker & Warburg, 1957
The Oath and other poems Giles Gordon, 1962
In Time of Crowding Brookside Press, 1975
In this Transparent Forest Green River Press, 1977
Outsing the Howling Permanent Press, 1979
The Fact of Music The Menard Press, 1980

TRANSLATIONS in book form of the following poets
Camoës (The Menard Press, 1976); Pessoa (Carcanet Press, 1971 and Penguin Books, 1974); Char, with M. A. Caws (Princeton University Press, 1976); Jorge de Sena (Mudborn Press, California, 1979); and Jean Mambrino (The Menard Press, 1979).